Beneath the Midi Sun

Beneath the Midi Sun

poems & images

Jim & Carol McCord

Shanti Arts Publishing
Brunswick, Maine

Beneath the Midi Sun

Copyright © 2021 Jim & Carol McCord

All Rights Reserved
No part of this book may be used or reproduced in any manner whatsoever without the written permission of the publisher.

Published by Shanti Arts Publishing
Interior and cover design by Shanti Arts Designs

Shanti Arts LLC
193 Hillside Road
Brunswick, Maine 04011
shantiarts.com

Printed in the United States of America

ISBN: 978-1-951651-50-3 (softcover)
ISBN: 978-1-951651-51-0 (hardcover)

Library of Congress Control Number: 2020946001

*For family and friends
in loving appreciation for being who you are*

CONTENTS

Acknowledgments 9

Out Our Back Window 11
Out Our Front Window 13

War in Heaven at Serrabona 14
Too Hard a Truth 16
Pope Innocent III 19
Rage of a Crusader 21
Defense of a Heretic 22
Cathar Dove 24
The Monks of Le Thoronet 27

Fire and Water 29
Villecroze 30
Eus 32
Country Dining 35
Ceret Market Day 37
Points of View 39
Last Days with the River Arc 40
Five Day Holiday 42

Morning 45
Peach Grove 47
Near the Visigoth Cemetery 48
Gray Matters 50
Revolution 53

Menhir 55
The So-called Deserted Village of Combes 57
Photograph of the River Lot 58
Land Clearing 60

Fine Work with Shears	63
Truffle Market	64
Bronze Portrait with Sunflowers	67
Vincent's Cypress and Olive	69
Eye View	71
At Le Pont de Montvert	73
No Known Address	74
Sunflowers	77
Seeing Round	78
Maillol's Girl Lounging	80
In La Chapelle Sainte Roseline	82
Rambler on the Midi Canal	85
Dolmen Huntress	87
Lavoir for Montsales	89
William Blake Visits Vincent van Gogh	91
Landscapes and Portraits	94
Wood and Glass	96
La Chapelle du Rosaire	99
Full House in Carcassonne	100
1833	102
Both Truths	105
First Snow	106
Unseasonable Winter in the Gard	108
Renoir's Last Years	110
Hard Rain	112
Saint-Pierre Cemetery	114
At Auvers-sur-Oise July 27, 1890	117
Stele with Cross of Lorraine	119
La Caunette in Minervois	121
Biographies	*123*

Acknowledgments

Our very special thanks to Annette LeClerc and Harry and Ginit Marten who have been exceedingly generous over many years helping us find the words and images that pair most happily to express what we intend. Special thanks, too, to Kelly Collett, Carl George, Peter Heinegg, David Kaczynski, Luis Martinez, Eric McCord, Shawne McCord, Daniel Payne, Jordan Smith, Charles Steckler, Ruth Stevenson, Bunkong Tuon, Malcolm Willison, and Sandy Wimer for their kind support and valued advice.

Out Our Back Window

Beyond the decorative patio
tiles, freshly painted black
railing, newly plastered
wall—beyond the garden
of raked pebbles, trimmed
shrubs, pruned fig—lie
shards of flower pots in
Gorgonian brambles among
stones from collapsed dry
walls. Over all a serene
rock face gazes. Its brow
rippled with age, scar
on right cheek, eyes the
homes for crag martins
to roost in darkness before
they take frenzied flight
to feast in day's light.

Out Our Front Window

The wall next door a hodge-podge of stones,
rocks, boulders, canal tiles, mortar.
Cracks splintered sharp as gutting knifes,
fissures like bolts of lightning, chinks
of darkness where light should be, hollows
with black bowels, hovels no bird dares
inhabit. All unhewn as the bed of our river
Cesse summer dry. Black, brown, tan, gray
with brick wedges the color of dried blood.

Below, our tidy courtyard and the entry gate
through which rode Simon de Montfort, butcher.
A Dominican fanatic with knife sharp as carbon
steel and no time to trim fat, no time to cut
cleanly a thigh from leg. Time only to gouge
out eyes of heretics, collect trophies of ears,
lips, tongues on his way up river to Minerve
to roast alive in the savage heat of July
one hundred sixty Cathars (more or less).

War in Heaven at Serrabona

for Peter

For this cosmic battle in pink marble
feathers and scales chafe, wings
and reptile bodies coil like volutes.
The dragon steady-eyed with sure
smile, arms like steel L braces.
Michael without sword or shield,
mouth gaped for air, eyes with fear.
The archangel here an old man
with full beard, more like father
than son, his bodily strength
failing, sense of duty shaken.

Too Hard a Truth

In pre-Romanesque fortress churches
no prayer can be answered in light.
When you pass through its oaken door
you must seal every chink of mortal
life, kneel and press palms until
senses numb, mind freezes, bone
fractures like ice. Do this full
of faith, you're told, and breath
breathes anew, heart opens, soul
takes flight from this aviary of night.

Pope Innocent III

in bejeweled vestments is innocent
as the beast with seven heads.
His churches like blue diamonds
where priests feast in great halls,
vow allegiances with tongues forked
like adders. Peace without a chance
in hell against his two-edged sword
that severs heads of schismatics.

Rage of a Crusader

Cathars pray in the synagogue of Satan.

Heretics who blaspheme with viper's tongue
our Roman Church, call it a den of thieves,
profess our priests copulate with the whore
of Babylon. They dare call Jehovah murderer,
our savior a harlot's lover, his body common
bread. Judases in fields of blood, their
Elect preach equality, their fornicators
chastity, their usurers poverty. We'll make
kindling of their tindery robes, flesh,
bones for radiant fires of damnation.

Defense of a Heretic

Our Cathar homes besieged by Catholic wolves.

We meet without ceremony in weaver's shops, speak civilly, abhor war. Sandals on our feet, coarse robes our clothing, our women and men equal. We eat what greens earth offers, drink what milk our animals give. Our tongues pure as wine from the grail at Montsegur. Jesus mortal, freed from Eucharist, Cross, the burden of forgiveness. Our bodies imprisoned, our prayers earthbound, our eternal souls reborn until our return to the starred light of heaven.

Cathar Dove

Ash from sheaths of straw,
wood stakes, robes, flesh, muscle, bone
flies free open-winged.

The Monks of Le Thoronet

worked and prayed, prayed and worked,
followed strict St. Benedict
as naturally as their monastery

followed its slope of land. Lives
distant from a world that devoured
souls whole, a refuge inside rough

walls with pure springs to nourish.
Hands-on in garden, mill, bakery;
hands pressed in silence for chapel.

No figure on their cross, no icons
to distract or weigh them down
beyond a few palms, water leaves,

flowers carved in the Chapter House.
Liturgical chants in their church
still echo off unadorned walls lit

by clear glass. Engineered simplicity
eight hundred years ago for light
to sing with stone, stone with light.

Fire and Water

A volcanic valley cut by no river,
its cliffs the exposed heart of split
faults. Underground, limestone soaks
up rain-fed streams to fill hollows
and caves, channels waters that weave
like cross-country runners to riverbeds.
Springs lose themselves in rivulets
or become life-giving fountains
for fields of maize and sunbaked
towns. Aquitania, the Romans named
the place, a land of waters seen
and unseen so unlike their yellow
Tiber, fortress walls, hunting gardens.

Villecroze

Water everywhere. Cascades
of silk tulle, pools to cool
young bodies, rivers to turn
dusty banks to mire. Streams
glide over rock step by step,
runnels channel to stone
aqueduct and through lavoir
where village women gather
for cabaret. Springs rise
to fill mouths of fountains.

So the jealous eye of Tavernes.
All waters there trapped
in subterranean darkness,
the navels of their women
worn to smooth nothings
by the edges of its wells.

Eus

for Michael and Richard

Our hill village
held together
dry rock on dry
rock zipper tight
and by mortar
troweled into rock
like a cocky suitor
who promises long
life and stability.

Plain fortress walls,
gaudy St. Vincent,
houses derelict
and modern all bedded
on boulders humped
like rhinos, smooth
as coat of gazelle,
edged with teeth
sharp as a tiger's.

Country Dining

for Howard

I'm not going to talk gourmet regional
cuisine—magret, cassoulet, boeuf
bourguignon, olive tapenade, crème
catalone—and I'm not sharing recipes.
I want to talk common fare and country
manners at Café de Pays where they serve
local wines to wash down local meat,
bread fresh from Le Pain Levain around
the corner, fruit plucked from nearby
orchards, greens from roadsides. Flavors
natural like aliment from paradise.

Mini breakfasts to savor at leisure,
two-hour lunches, four-hour dinners. Food
never fast where owners in jeans greet
you with the warmth of an old friend,
offer you the table of your choice. Where
two servers attentive as sentinels care
for four dozen diners, and water and bread
arrive in a blink. Where aperitif relaxes,
wine refreshes, entrée takes the edge off,
plat fills, dessert soothes, espresso
and lively conversation settle all.

To top it off: no bill arrives till asked
for, no "do you want change," no doggie bag.

Ceret Market Day

for Sandy and Denny

It's often hard to tell
the master from the dog,
the vendor from the wares.

This morning a yogurt girl tiny as her jar,
Catalan butcher with sausage fingers,
stuffed ravioli woman and crusty baker.

Oval-faced poulter with beak for nose,
cheesy husband and creamy wife,
sweet flipper of savory crepes.

Fruiterer with orange complexion,
greengrocer with head like lettuce,
bottle-shaped vintner well-corked.

Pin-sharp seamstress thin as thread,
Shaggy shoe hawker in fuzzy slippers,
king-size man on queen-size mattress.

Points of View

His walking cane beating the moonlit
air, Cezanne railed young Emil
Bernard about plans by surveyors
to line ancient streets with
sidewalks, straighten his town.
Changes to deafen past harmony.

Shops, houses, chimneys must match
the upright bell-tower at Gardonne
for windmills to eye with pleasure.
No offal or lignite mines allowed.
Bernard listens patiently, treads
lightly, sees the old man "so tired."

The bell-tower now stands a curio
beside steaming cauldrons, retching
stacks, cement power posts catching
light the church now gone once caught.
In the distance Mont Sainte-Victoire
supine in haze lies flayed of woodlands.

Last Days with the River Arc

for Ginit

It was play when Cezanne and Zola swam
as boys in this river, skipped stones
over ripples Monet would have loved
to paint. It was hard work for the old
man seated hunched on its cool bank
the last blistering summer of his life,
hump-backed bridge above a scythe
to set aquiver leaves of trees and blue,
yellow, violet brushwood at river's edge.

In his atelier in Aix on a mechanical
easel those trees anchored in that bank
become an arbor to shade a community
of women at lavation, their bodies angled
like pines swaying above summer waters.

The first nature, the second art.
Both white heat to the painter.

Five Day Holiday

When Arles and its river dulled,
Van Gogh took a cheap mail coach
to Saintes-Maries-de-la-Mer in search
of colors stirred by sea and air.

His eye caught lavender fields,
white dwellings under steep roofs
of orange and purple, village girls
who recalled Cimabue and Giotto.

The sea for him an ever-changing
mackerel he never knew for sure
glinted green or purple or blue,
tinted pink or gray from shifts in light.

In *Barques de peche* four boats lounge
on warm sands, masts and spars akimbo,
tillers and sails at rest, sea and sky
thinly brushed Mediterranean blue.

In *Paysage marin* two fishing boats
with sails filled by Mistral wind
battle a sea of cobalt and black
cresting and breaking yellow and green.

Views to remind us, perhaps, wherever
we go we take with us our twofold self.

Morning

for Eric and Kelly

Sun washes valley,
mourning doves mimic church bells,
stones warm, mists dissolve.

Peach Grove

Buds bring promise,
fruit fulfillment,
blossoms the truth
of short-lived beauty
when orchards rage
in pollinated frenzy.

Near the Visigoth Cemetery

for Annette

Supple vineyards
in undulant fields.

Streams nimble,
rivers graceful.

Lithe pines
sway with ease.

Landscape lissome
as a ballerina.

Gray Matters

An untouched photograph
in color without a trace
of primary red, blue, green.
Scrubland of steel wool,
forests of wrought iron,
pewter peak. Sky of smoke
ember above pearl river
of cloud. The beauty of
grays to calm, to sooth.

Revolution

This outbuilding a hierarchy
of rock and wood, slate and
ceramic tile. Foundation
stones locked in implacable
place, ash doors strong as
slabs of concrete, mortar
hard as soldered rail track.
Above, interlocked roof lip
secures tiles lapped for a
garden of moss, lichen, weed.

Half way up an insubordinate
fern escapes green as youth
out a broken vent window.

Menhir

for Shawne

You're one of the lucky ones
not to freeze in Ireland
every cold-bound winter.
Consider yourself blessed
to bask in the warm Midi
south where healthful air
breathes with ease to assure
a less pitted complexion.
I see you an ancient relic
with lost past well pleased
to share common company
with rows of baby vines
and white field flowers
to tickle your feet.

The So-called Deserted Village of Combes

Euphorbia springs from a cornucopia of boulders,
button-size star flowers stud shrubland,
sheep and goats nose spring-fresh crabgrass.

Mountain air refreshes empty doorways, window frames
hold mouthfuls of sun. A solitary fir shades
the brawny shepherd with belly round as a pumpkin,

his caravan immaculate as a spinster's
cottage, his dog keen-eyed as the harrier
overhead, his flock hardy as horses of Mérens.

Only the restored church is out of place,
as unnatural here as a Pope's jeweled mitre
or fearfully symmetrical garden.

Photograph of the River Lot

West of Cajarc the river
bends hard as a horseshoe
into this second of three
oxbows. In early morning
mist the photograph—
no matter how true—
can never match the eye
of the photographer
that itself shifts focus
like a shutterbug
with heart aflutter.

The result: branches
of foreground ash keener
than they are, distant
haze not as mysterious.
Sky brighter in the river
than above hills, fields
like fleece more than grass.
As solitary as that tree
in the field, both camera
and the eye behind it view
find through their own lens.

Land Clearing

Backhoe with armored yellow torso
cranes its neck like a bloodthirsty
dinosaur, mouths a boulder with
portcullis teeth (rich soil dripping
from its jaws), places it at field's
edge as if a jewel on gemologist's
cushion, then nudges it into precise
position, caresses it with a tap,
purrs with pleasure like a kitten.

Fine Work with Shears

Trained trunks with two arms
equidistant from each other
sweep in picture perfect rows
like rail tracks from roadside
to impenetrable woodlands.
In paths of clay and sandstone
a husband and wife full-bodied
as their dark red wine prune vines,
quick-snip without mercy stems
of doubtful character, cut
errant tails of spurs back to three
chosen buds for broad summer leaves
to catch sun, for fruit to stain
lips. Their labor easeful in this
warm demi-Eden of little rain
and strong winds where eugenics
flourishes free of moral qualm.

Truffle Market

Nosed from under leaf litter
by the snout of hogs and looking
more like turds than diamonds
of the kitchen, these black
tubers most fragrant in winter
sniffed as if Romanée-Conti
by Parisian restaurateurs,
fondled like puppies by women
in Hermes gloves, offered
by old men in threadbare
shirts with hands earth-worn.

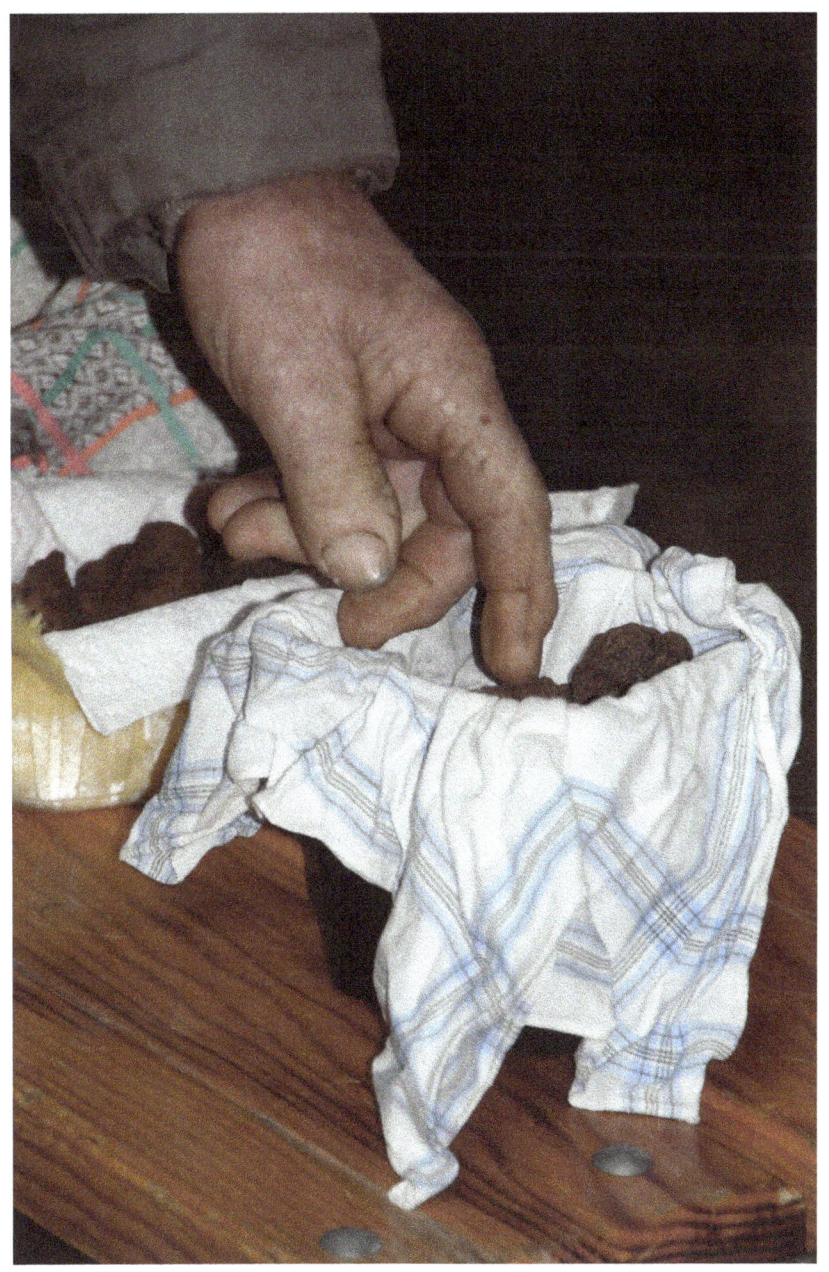

Bronze Portrait with Sunflowers

Van Gogh cast mid-step walking
to his room with kill in hands.
Brows knit, corners of his mouth
downcast like the sunflowers
he carries. There can be no honest
acceptance of his act, his heart
despondent at how the flowers must
pay for his art. Right hand fingers
one gently, its seeded head weary
of time bent toward the ground.
Left hand grips four stalks cut
razor clean, their heads cradled
in his arm catching last breath.
In the studio he'll arrange them
artfully, give them a glory
they never had in fields, turn
fading yellow petals with sun spots
into solar flares of paint. But
here a split second caught for
a monochrome tribute to both flowers
and painter who die like stars.

Vincent's Cypress and Olive

Why do you paint cypress one day
and olive the next? Tap-rooted
spear heads with tapered tips,
then dancers sporting afros
studded with sequins? Black
as green can be for one, silver,
blue, bronze, violet, gray-green
commingled for the other?

There is, of course, some common
ground. Neither blossoms like peach
or almond, iris or lavender, and I
notice you paint both from a distance,
as if they were wannabe friends
you feared to know too closely,
or with whom you might be tempted
to share too much of yourself.

Eye View

In the park a natural theater
with seats of rock and stage
of grass. Human history played
and replayed summer after summer.
Parasol pines shade restless
children, watchful parents,
family dogs from the searing sun.
Encircling cypress cast shadows
sharp as lances. Pines shape
themselves, cypress shaped
by electric hand saws. One tree
protects, the other arouses
fear, incites contempt.

At Le Pont de Montvert

Spring waters of the Tarn don't
give a damn for anything human.
They can-can over boulders,
tickle steps in their midriffs,
polish pebbles white, streak rocks
blood red, rest flag blue in pools.

River free as the French dream
of liberty to go its own natural
way while clock tower and humpback
bridge look on, their footings
in block stone resoled again
and again over four centuries.

No Known Address

> *"No one is allowed to touch me . . . no one will get their claws into me! Never! Never!"*
> —Paul Cezanne to Emile Bernard

As a man of feeling:

an aborted seedling,
a stalk blighted by cicadas,
a vine crippled from black measles,
a tree tented with moths,
a woodland struck down by blows from Mistral winds.

Draw, eat, paint, sleep.
Swim in colors, dive out of touch.

Sunflowers

> "... it is better to be a sheep than a wolf, better to
> be slain than slay—better to be Abel than Cain."
> —Vincent van Gogh

Giddy for Gauguin to arrive, van Gogh
blind to all but sunflowers. White walls
of his studio plastered with yellows
to blot out blues pale as the damned
on St. Trophime, dark as royal robes
in its stained-glass windows. Earthen
pots and bouquets in vases painted over
and over to find simplicity in repetition.
Living wheels of fire spinning ochre
and chrome yellow into gold and satin.

Gauguin called them a "perfect page,"
Vincent called them rustic symbols
of gratitude. After two months of rough
brotherhood, petals blanch, stems char,
corolla explodes with manic cries.

Seeing Round

No straight lines, no angles, no sharp
edges for Maillol. Torsos round and
heavy as Plain trees in Banyuls-sur-Mer,
arms strong as those of women at lavoir,
thighs like breakwater boulders, breasts
small and firm as grapes in his vineyard,
hair coiffed in buns. Backs arch like
the ridges of the hills he loved to walk,
bodies flow like sea swells in the bay
and like the stream below his mountain home
that's smoothed for centuries rough-edged
stones. To mark his grave *La Mediterranean*
mourns the man who made her, the world
at war, 60 million bodies turned dust.

Maillol's Girl Lounging

for Jillmarie

Feminine beauty
frozen in bronze, warmed by sun,
haunted by shadows.

In La Chapelle Sainte Roseline

Roseline a wily child to sneak
bread from her wealthy father's
pantry for local paupers starving
at his gate. Wile then transformed
to miracle when stolen rolls
in her apron turn roses, petals
flutter like manna to the ground.
No arranged marriage for her, life
to be lean as her frame with visions
of mortification to sustain.

Five years after death her exhumed
body fresh as a scarlet rose, eyes
crystalline and bright as rubies,
gold headband untarnished. Her body
today lies silent as her Carthusian
vow on view in a glass coffin.
White robe and black shawl flow
over flesh grained like wood,
her face like burl, fingers
and toes like charred twigs.

On a wall nearby Chagall's mosaic
Repast of the Angels relieves
the shame she felt the morning
she set no table for her sisters.
Three angels deliver platters
of fish and fowl, bowls of fruit,
a vase of flowers, carafe of wine.
A dove above leaves its bouquet
nest to fly sunward. Tiles like
gemstones sprinkled with gold dust.

Rambler on the Midi Canal

She's no engineer or commercial
adventurer but knows what a genius
Mssr. Riquet, hydrologist nonpareil.
She also knows of the thousands
who pickaxed and shoveled the way,
lime-pointed stone, laid brick,
fired forge. 150 miles, 63 locks,
126 bridges, 55 aqueducts, 6 dams.

On the towpath she eyes yellow irises,
fingers rushes, scowls at loosestrife,
passes diseased Plane trees to be felled
for striplings of turkey oak that one
day will hold banks in place. She soft-
shoes around bends of the ever-shifting
waterway, its hushed waters prismatic
one moment, reflective gray the next.

Dolmen Huntress

for Carol

She's off again this morning
armed with phone to track rocks
on Minerve's limestone plateau,
find every tiny amphora icon
on her GPS screen. Above gorge
and beyond vineyards kermes oak,
shrubby boxwood, and asphodel
go unnoticed; scents of thyme,
lavender, orchid waft too subtle
for her to trace. She has no
interest in raptors overhead
or hints of boar on the path.

Her passion simply bare-bones
of stone, the ways they stand,
lean, have fallen. Ceremonial
sites stripped naked of tumulus,
chambers hollowed of artifacts,
capstones seemingly lifted by
goliaths. She can never know
the people or why they labored
like oxen five thousand years ago
to anchor each megalith, set
in place each block. Praise be
the mysteries of rock and man.

Lavoir for Montsales

On laundry day maids, wives, widows
with wicker baskets filled over crowns
stepped the steep, narrow path to this
lone niche of Flancou valley, leaving
behind men, duties of home, the string
of crosses that descend from village
to cemetery as icons of sacrifice.

A woman's public place to wash sheets,
skirts, collarless shirts and chat loud
as a crow's caw or soft as a dove's coo.
Today pond and building unused, lock
blocks broken, gate rusted. The only sound
crystalline water trickling from source
to stream with no need to stain it clear.

William Blake Visits Vincent van Gogh

The match was natural. Two
fiery red heads who scorched
earth with their paintings.
Blake in van Gogh's Yellow House
felt a familiar comfort in its
small rooms with picture frames
rubbing against each other.
The two shared drinks at the Café
Terrace under ghastly light.
Whores and homeless worked
streets of Arles like those
in Lambeth. Charter'd Rhone
flowed like Thames waters.
Cornfields of polished brass
reminded Blake of boyhood walks,
starry nights of angels singing
hallelujah. Imagination,
they agreed, has nothing to do
with memory. There were no skies
littered with black crows until
talk turned testy in the hospital.

Blake: All depends on outline.
Van Gogh: All depends on color.

Blake: All depends on where lights and darks are put.
Van Gogh: All depends on where colors are put.

Blake: Oil sullies color like any cloggy vehicle.
Van Gogh: Oil gives strength to color. *— continued*

Blake: Firm and determinate lineaments are gratified desire.
Van Gogh: Firm and determinate lineaments are frustrated desire.

Blake: Clear and precise execution is art.
Van Gogh: Uncontrolled emotion is art.

Blake: The clearer the imaginative organ, the more distinct the object.
Van Gogh: The clearer the imaginative organ, the more dynamic nature.

Blake: Natural objects always deaden and obliterate imagination in man.
Van Gogh: Natural objects are in imaginative harmony with man.

Blake: You have narrow, blinking eyes.
Van Gogh: Your eyes are blinded by Gnostic dogma.

Blake: You are no artist, but a heathen philosopher at enmity against all true art and inspiration.

Van Gogh pulls a razor.
Blake retreats into vision.

Landscapes and Portraits

> *"One must have ambition to succeed,
> and ambition seems to me absurd."*
> —Vincent van Gogh

Maybe not ambition for fame or fortune,
Vincent, but how ambitious to tackle all
fitful nature has to offer with pencil,
pen, and paint. From tender peach tree
to spiteful *le mistral*, from a young
girl's hushed grace to a postman's
surety of self. Your impassioned fires
of eye and heart no reason could allay.
So your colors speak as words, skies
whorl in cosmic space, locals pose
in rooms decorated with obstinacy.

Wood and Glass

St. Bernard chapel on the manicured
grass grounds of Fondation Maeght
is not so austere as the saint would
have liked. Nonetheless, he stands
like a sentry outside chiseled in stone
and thought for the wooden man inside.
Christ unblemished. Body pristine, head
without a trace of thorns, face tranquil
in sleep deep as understanding. Braque's
dove flies above toward the waning moon,
barely clears our natural world of tree
in leaf, flower bed, pot of shoots.

La Chapelle du Rosaire

No stained glass in narrow niches perched
high to brighten rough stone for Matisse.
To the south frosted yellow fronds hold
the viewer's spirit inside while translucent
sky blues and garden greens stream through
bars black as jail railings to illumine
chapel floor all hours of day, all seasons.

Only in winter do sprays of blended color
caress three faceless figures on the wall
opposite. Studies reduced to black lines
straight as his charcoal-tipped sticks,
curved as petals. Saint Dominic with book,
mother and child made flesh from text. One
word, "AVE," sings welcome and farewell.

On the east wall a jumbled leave-taking.
Tortured body, composition of fourteen
stations as one. Jesus whole, broken, halved,
quartered; hunched, grounded, pinned, laid
to rest. A number for each step splashed on
as if an afterthought. In the west the Tree
of Life with radiant blossoms on cactus stems.

Full House in Carcassonne

for Pattie

The audience of shadowed seats
still, silent, mesmerized
by a stage filled with nothing.
No curtain, no props, no feisty
pre-teen on balcony or love-struck
boy below to speak words that tumble
like unskilled acrobats from his heart.
No palazzos where families poison
their children with hateful tongues,
no swashbuckling firebrands in town
square. No nurse or apothecary to cure
the malady. Shadows of seats in perfect
lines perfectly spaced and fixed
like tongues in grooves. Every spectral
spectator desperate to see more
than the tragic nothing they imagine,
more than their dark, uniform selves.

1833

for Chris and Jo

Modest houses in this village
began with caves behind oak doors.
Sacred paintings of mammoths,
figurines of fertile women,
engraved shells, pottery, beads,
hints of origins nowhere seen.
These unnatural grottos
built with hard day labor

to support the lit dwelling
above. Homes raised by hand
from dusty earth to tiled roof.
Stone from causse, beams from
prickled valley sides lugged
by horse and man, their steps
slowed by the weight of the load,
their breath heavy from toil.

Upstairs this dark winter day
a pin-shaft of light through a
Lilliputian window catches our
breadboard scored with cuts
and deep gouges. Its single
knot like the eye of a storm
radiates oaken rings as if
echoing the history of place.

Both Truths

for Andy

Two mountain quarries,
marble and lime rock.

One mined for beauty,
other fired for use.

That is all you need
to know of earth.

First Snow

The sky a dull sheet of steel
lighter than gunmetal, darker
than our village road. Uniform,
immobile, touching nothing,
moving nothing, detached. Eyes
blank, pale as pearl, cold.

From inside I watch porch-lit
flakes fall like stars and land
like space ships, the spent orchard
turn from flat sea bed to swells.
Only thin window panes separate
allure and stifled desire.

Unseasonable Winter in the Gard

No sunburnt mirth. Lamp
light iced, tiles shocked, plaster walls
suffering chilblains.
Feathered pines on Les Castels
eye gray skies like snowy owls.

Renoir's Last Years

In a rare film clip the old painter rides
his wheelchair beside youngest son, his yap
telling where he's jabbed the brush and maybe
why. Smoke from his nostrils steams like
the train down the hill. Body thin as a twig,
animated as a flip book. With help, his brush
in and out of hand, his cigarette lit. Hands
like talons mummified. Stones for knuckles,
fingers gnarled like trunk and leader
of the ancient olive tree in his orchard.

A body in love with fleshy women and children
well-dressed, well-behaved, trapped in fashion.

Hard Rain

There's no need to glorify Cezanne's death,
repeat his vow to die with brush in hand.
As he feared, reason simply failed.
Not possible, he'd written, to practice
theories out of doors in rainy season,
but there he sat for hours at his motif,
eyes straining to raise fallen lines,
untangle overlapping plains. Autumn
rain showered him like poison pellets.

He likely did not feel the indignity
of his return home in a laundry cart
or loss of his terror of touch when
two men eased him into bed. Breath
hard, coughs often, mind as empty
as the untouched squares in all
the paintings he'd leave unfinished.

Saint-Pierre Cemetery

Cezanne lies one of nine in a two-family
tomb, his name and dates incised without
distinction to match mother and father.
Thick-limbed pines to the west allow only
a splinter of light on the lid of stone.
The Roman family presses close on the right,
the plot to the left abandoned. A grave
one aisle east holds the bones of triple-
titled Barthelemy Niollon, a once-known
academic painter. The lofty monument
in which he rests blocks Cezanne's sight
of the sun as it rises to caress
the body of Sainte-Victoire.

At Auvers-sur-Oise July 27, 1890

The second after van Gogh's body
welcomed the bullet, I'd like
to believe mind-vexing dualities
and his anguished desire for
serenity dissolved in the heat
and energy of a sulfurous sun.
Rock ravines, cypresses, wheat
fields, sowers, black crows lost
to flashes of light. All color
bleached. No red vineyards, no
silvery olive trees, no purple
irises, no vermilion poppies,
no golden sunflowers. All white
until a blackness dark as his room
colored his death and life.

Stele with Cross of Lorraine

This marker about his height

beside a dirt road in his Black Mountains.
Julien Vignon resistance fighter with mind
nimble as a red fox, body strong as a brown
bear, will like a stag with antlers locked
until stalked by Nazis under an August sun
hot as a German 88. His thickset cedars,
sheltering oaks and ash could not shield him
from the Luger. Advice more than solace
left for passersby: "Courage is to love
life and look on death with a calm eye."

La Caunette in Minervois

for Caroline and Trevor

That boy of twelve with his backpack outside the medieval gate of La Carambelle is—by right of birth and place—free from thoughts of fear or hope. His village smothered one century would catch its breath the next. Its mine for low grade lignite coal fed Nazi war machines, today organic wine quenches the thirst of tourists. The boy weaned on open skies and deep gorges, raised among stone walls once roofed, windowed, doored with iron hinges. An explorer of rock cliffs with prehistoric caves of ash pits and animal bone. A trekker through valleys rich with vineyards where woodlands, olive trees, fields of goats used to be. His river sings its melodies to him each season: in parched summer when waters hide underground from the blistering sun, in chilled winter, during fall floods, spring surges. Natural and human history in this mite of a village make for an even heartbeat that rests with ease deep in marrow. The boy has no need to trouble himself with understanding or accepting life or death, no need to believe there's more to living than living.

Biographies

Jim McCord is an emeritus professor of English literature whose poems have appeared in a variety of journals and four books.

Carol McCord is a lifelong hiker and former yoga instructor. Her photographs have been selected for exhibitions and publications in the United States and abroad.

Shanti Arts

Nature • Art • Spirit

Please visit us online
to browse our entire book catalog,
including poetry collections and fiction,
books on travel, nature, healing, art,
photography, and more.

Also take a look at our highly
regarded art and literary journal,
Still Point Arts Quarterly, which
may be downloaded for free.

www.shantiarts.com

www.ingramcontent.com/pod-product-compliance
Lightning Source LLC
Chambersburg PA
CBHW042134160426
43199CB00022B/2915